PLYMOUTH PL5 3EQ
33 CHAUCER WAY, MANADON
SOCIAL SERVICES
ST. BUDEAUX/HONICKNOWLE

From the moment the tree house was completed, 11-year-old Pat's life got complicated. First those abominable boys — her brothers and Sam — carried their teasing to new extremes. But Pat almost forgot them when flashing lights and a crumbling house presented her with a real mystery to solve. Finally some new ideas about selfishness cap her series of adventures.

PICKED-ON
PAT

PICKED-ON PAT

Written by Aleda Renken
Art by Michael Norman

A Haley Adventure Book

Publishing House
St. Louis

Concordia Publishing House, St. Louis, Missouri

Copyright © 1973 Concordia Publishing House
Library of Congress Catalog Card No. 73-75864
ISBN 0-570-03601-1

MANUFACTURED IN THE UNITED STATES OF AMERICA

3 4 5 6 7 8 9 10 11 12   DB   90 89 88 87 86 85 84 83 82 81

CHAPTER 1

Pat slapped five sheets of torn wax paper on the kitchen counter. On each square she flipped a slice of bread. In less than a minute each piece of bread had a teaspoon of soft jelly in the center. Working fast, she put a hunk of peanut butter on top of the jelly. With flying fingers she covered the mixture with another slice of bread, then wrapped them. They did look like sandwiches. Pat liked the assembly-line way of making sandwiches. No wonder Henry Ford could make so many cars, way back there somewhere in history. Besides, this was a very special occasion, and the boys would be too excited to notice whether the insides of the sandwiches were in big hunks in the middle of the bread or not. The tree house was finally finished!

The Haley children were going to celebrate its completion by having a lunch inside the tree house, high up among the strong horizontal limbs of the big oak. It was a wonderful time to be in an oak tree because the baby leaves were just coming out and were not green but a soft delicate pink. In fact, all the oak woods looked like a fairyland of pink lace.

Since they'd moved to the country, Sam,

the neighbor boy, had taught them a lot of ways to have fun. Sam had lived there with his grandmother since he was three years old. His mother was dead, and his father was an entertainer who played at different night clubs across the country all winter. But his dad did take him on vacations almost every summer and also gave him some expensive presents. The latest had been a ten-speed bike that would have turned the Haley children green with envy had it not been that Sam considered that anything given to him was also given to the Haleys. To the children Sam was another member of the family except they never fought with him. Sam was no fighting person. If he didn't agree with what was said, he just looked far away with cool blue eyes that seemed to forget anyone was around.

He had worked hard on the tree house and had furnished a lot of material from an old barn of Granny's. He was with Pat's brothers in the tree house now, waiting for the lemonade and sandwiches. Pat started to get down five glasses but remembered in time that she would have to wash them. Instead she found some slightly used paper cups, rinsed them, and tossed them in the sack.

On her way to the woods, Pat paused to admire some tiny white flowers that she was certain had grown in the short time it had taken her to make the lunch. How timid they seemed, quivering in the soft breeze! And they weren't the only pretty hints all around her that spring would soon be there. It made her feel warm and excited.

There hadn't been many introductions to the changes in seasons where they lived in the city. It was winter, so you got out your last year's winter coat. It was spring, so you got out your last year's spring coat. It was summer, so you got out your shorts. And fall. Well, fall just seemed to slip in without anyone really knowing, especially since there were no trees around their neighborhood. But Sam said that fall in Missouri was the most gorgeous season of all.

But even though Pat loved the country, she did miss having girl friends living near. That was her one regret in leaving the city. Her three brothers and Sam just didn't take the place of the two girls who had lived in the same apartment house. Although Pat had to admit that there had been some vicious fights among her and her girl friends. Some of those battles turned into cold wars when they didn't speak to each other for days.

Pat had almost reached the foot of the homemade ladder. She wished they could have had television coverage. After all, this was as important to the Haleys and Sam as the moon walk. She could see herself in one of those new belted sport coats, turning to wave to the viewing audience as she reached the top step.

"Hey, someone come down and help me! I can't climb the ladder with my arms full," she yelled.

There was a sudden silence in the tree house and not one head appeared at the house opening.

Then Pat saw the freshly painted sign.

"No Girls Permited."

"Hey, you forgot one 't,'" she said, and then the words hit her. Girls! Did they mean . . . ? But they didn't dare leave *her* out. She'd done more work on that tree house than all of the boys put together. Her hands still ached with bruises, and she had a splinter as big as a telephone pole embedded in her best thumb.

Still no sound from above. She could imagine what was going on up there. Sam would be staring straight ahead with that half-smile Pat had seen on the faces of Buddhas at the museum. Donnie's eyes would be bulging, waiting for food. Jeff would look uneasy and Kurt would be waiting for her to blow her top like she did so often when the boys teased her.

Well, she wouldn't! She'd stay cool and very polite. She took a deep gulp of air and said in her sweetest tones, "What's with this sign, boys?"

"You can read, can't you?" Kurt's voice came out with a squeak as it usually did lately.

"You mean, . . . " She had to take another deep breath. "You mean, I'm not *allowed* up there?"

"It's a *boys'* club, Pat," Jeff explained.

"Did you bring the lunch and lemonade?" Donnie was only six, but his appetite was way ahead of his years.

Pat ignored him. "Boys' club! You've let me slave and work on this thing for six months, and now I'm not allowed to come up?" In spite of herself, her voice got a little higher with each word.

"Read the constitution, Mr. Secretary," Kurt ordered.

There was some whispering. Then Sam in a very soft voice began: "Section four, page five, 'No girls permitted on the premises.' "

That did it! Not only the words but the fact that Sam who usually was on her side was now going along with her brothers. How dared he let himself be brainwashed like that?

"Sam," she said weakly, "Is this the rule?"

"The supreme majority . . ." Sam began in his soft voice, but that was enough. It seemed to Pat that her ears exploded after those words.

"You, you cheats!" she screamed.

Through the angry roaring in her ears she heard Kurt. "Because of your work, you may have one girl friend here for an afternoon, if the members agree."

Pat lost all control. She grabbed in the sack and hurled a sandwich at the sign. The top slice of bread fell off, and a glob of peanut butter smashed on the word "girls" and covered it completely.

"Cheats! Cheats!" she sobbed and ran down the path through the woods. Donnie's little pup, Poochie, thought it was a good game and stayed right at her heels.

Pat jumped across the creek and tore up the hill. There was an old mulberry tree with limbs so low they almost touched the ground. She had found a comfortable seat on one of those limbs, and this is where she went when she was hurt or angry. From here she could see the river and the woods and, far off, the roofs of houses where the town nestled in the greening trees.

Not that she saw anything that day. It seemed to her that steam must be coming out of her ears, nose, and mouth from all the boiling inside. Her brothers! Kurt, Jeff, and Donnie had ganged up on her again and even had the nerve to talk Sam into it. She'd *never* forgive them. Just let them pack their own lunches from now on. She was *through*.

Pat wondered what her dad and mother would say about that so-called constitution.

And they *would* hear about it, she would see to that. Why did there have to be a constitution for a tree house anyway? If only a big windstorm would come up and blow that house out of the tree — clear out of the county — and with the boys in it!

Pat glanced guiltily at the sky, almost afraid she'd see a funnel cloud on the horizon. She really shouldn't have wished anything as bad as that. Besides as many nails as they had put in the tree she doubted very much whether a tornado could budge it. Nail after nail they'd hammered into that poor tree. She began to wonder if nails hurt trees.

Suddenly Pat realized her angry feelings toward the boys were cooling off. She didn't want that to happen. She had a *right* to be angry. It was so awfully unfair, and Pat hated unfairness, especially to herself.

She slid from the tree limb and started to run down the hill. Her mother would be home soon, and then Pat could really get herself all steamed up again. She had a nice feeling of satisfaction as she rehearsed her story. Oh, she would be very careful to stay with the truth!

Pat was halfway down the hill when she remembered the sack of sandwiches and the thermos jug she'd left under the tree. Wearily she climbed back up the hill. She didn't mind leaving those lousy sandwiches — the little wild animals would have a feast on them—but her mother would be angry if she left the jug.

At the top of the hill she saw Poochie running and barking frantically at something that seemed to flutter for an instant in the bushes and trees and then disappear.

"Poochie, you come here!" she ordered. The pup gave one more bark and trotted to her. "Aren't you ashamed to be chasing a poor little rabbit or . . . " Pat stopped. Come to think of it, that flutter of red (or was it brown?) couldn't have been either of those animals. She shrugged. What difference did it make? She went over to the big mulberry tree to pick up the thermos and sandwich bag. They were gone!

Pat rubbed her eyes and looked in the tall grass. This was where she had dropped them when she had climbed into the tree. Could Poochie really have been chasing an animal? But the idea of a squirrel or rabbit running away with a big red thermos and a sandwich sack was too much to swallow. She saw the round of flattened grass where the jug had stood. Ah! The boys must have seen her leave and come up to get the sandwiches and lemonade. Her anger flared again, and she ran down the hill.

Near the creek she saw Sam's Granny cutting weeds with a small paring knife. Granny looked up, her warm brown eyes twinkling as usual. Sam shared her with the Haleys as he shared everything he loved.

"Want to come to eat supper with us?" she asked, straightening her back as if to rest it.

Pat looked at the basket of green leaves. "You having weeds for supper?"

"No, these are spring greens. They're called lamb's-quarter, and they're delicious. Why don't you come and eat with us?"

"Because I've something I have to talk about to my family." Pat's green eyes were flashing. "I'm sure I'd love the lamb's-whatever-it-is stuff, but ask me again sometime."

Granny's eyes were keen, so keen that sometimes Pat was sure they could X-ray right through bone and skin into your very brain. "You're mad about something." Granny didn't really ask, she stated it.

"Yes, I am," Pat admitted, lifting her chin proudly.

"At the boys again?"

"Yes."

Granny began cutting leaves again, humming tonelessly under her breath, so Pat knew she wasn't really too interested in the fight with the boys.

"You didn't see any of the boys go to the hill and bring back a sack and thermos jug, did you?" she asked.

"No," replied Granny. "But I haven't been

here very long. I heard them talking in the tree house when I went by."

Pat turned toward home. After all, the boys could have gone up the hill on the other side and gotten the bag and jug. She smiled to herself. She was *glad* the sandwiches were messy. And from now on there wouldn't be any sandwiches at all for the boys. Not from her!

CHAPTER 2

Mrs. Haley was peeling potatoes at the sink. She was not much taller than Pat, but her hair was a rich dark mahogany while Pat's was nearer the shade of carrots. They both had deep green eyes. Pat hoped that someday her hair would darken like her mother's, but as yet it had not changed one shade. She knew because she cut a wisp each month and compared it with the previous month's wisp.

"Where are the boys?" Mrs. Haley asked.

"In the tree house."

"And why aren't you there?"

"Because they wouldn't allow me to set one foot on the ladder now that the place is finished." Pat went to the sink and splashed cold water on her flushed face. She felt like she was beginning to steam again.

Her mother's lips tightened as she handed Pat a towel. "Patricia Haley, are you fighting with your brothers again?"

"I didn't fight. I ran away up to the hill. Mom . . . " Pat had to stop to steady her voice. "There was a sign on the ladder, and it said, 'No Girls Permited.' I know Jeff wrote it because his spelling is lousy, and there was only one 't' in 'permitted.'"

Mrs. Haley threw a potato in a pan of water. "We'll talk about it when your father comes home. Now, set the table, and don't just sling the silverware around, please."

The boys came in soon afterward, but they said nothing to Pat.

"Where's the thermos?" she asked Donnie who was the last to come in.

"You took it with you, and you know it. You took the lunch too, and that wasn't very nice." Donnie was very reproachful.

Mrs. Haley turned from the stove. "What did you do with the jug, Pat?"

"I put it under the mulberry tree. After I started home, I remembered and went back after it, but it was gone and so was the sack of sandwiches."

"Maybe Granny took it home. You know how she feels about wasting anything. She probably gave those sandwiches to her chickens."

"No, she didn't, because I saw her and talked to her, and she wasn't going up the hill at all."

"You'll look for it in the morning," Mrs. Haley said, "and if you don't find it, you'll get another one out of your allowance. You should learn to be more careful."

Pat said nothing, but she was very unhappy. A new jug would take over half her allowance, and she had already borrowed some money from Jeff to get herself one of the new bracelets all the girls were wearing.

She didn't know when her mother had time to tell Dad about the fight, but there was something in the way he acted that made Pat sure he knew. The boys must have had the same feeling because they were unusually quiet all through dinner and kept stealing uncertain looks at Pat.

After dinner Mr. Haley rose from the table and looked at all of them. "We're having a meeting in the recreation room as soon as the dishes are done. Who is on duty tonight, Mother?"

Mrs. Haley looked at the bulletin board above the sink where she kept the weekly job allotments posted.

"Kurt and Jeff tonight. Pat and Donnie tomorrow."

Pat loved her little brother, but he really must have been the slowest dish dryer in the whole history of the human race. While he often made her laugh with his crazy conversation, it took him one whole story to dry a single cup.

"Maybe Mom won't cook so much tomorrow evening, and we won't have so many dishes," Donnie consoled when he saw her mouth droop.

Pat nodded absently and went upstairs to

study math. But somehow all she could put her mind to was the speech she intended to make about the ban on her membership in the club. When a big family problem came up, they had a court hearing where each member could state his case. Mr. Haley was the judge and Mrs. Haley was the jury of one. When Pat was called downstairs, all three boys were lined up on the divan. She took a seat on the opposite side of the room.

"Patricia, I understand you were not permitted in the tree house," Mr. Haley began.

"That's right."

"Why not?"

"Because I'm being discriminated against, because I'm a girl." This was to be only her opening statement, but before she could go on, her father turned to the boys.

"Is this true?"

Pat knew that Kurt would do the talking because he was the oldest and the mouthiest. He cleared his throat to be sure he was going to sound like a man instead of a mouse.

"Our constitution is drawn up so that it's a stag club. Like a men's club, Dad." His voice had started deep and important but ended up with a rusty break that made Donnie giggle.

Mr. Haley gave Donnie a stern look, and Donnie smothered his laugh with a big bite of cookie that he took out of his shirt pocket.

"And you voted on this?"

"Yes, sir."

"And where was Pat while you were drawing up this . . . this document?"

Kurt flushed. "She was . . . well . . . she was getting a lunch to celebrate the end of the construction."

"I see." Mr. Haley took a pencil from his pocket and turned it thoughtfully between his fingers. "Nothing was said about this restriction of girls while the tree house was being built, I gather?"

"N . . . no."

"How does Sam feel about this?"

Pat leaned forward eagerly. How did Sam feel about her not being a club member? Mr. Haley looked at Jeff.

"I really don't think it made too much difference to Sam." Jeff avoided Pat's eyes. "I think the fun to Sam was in the building. He didn't care too much about a club. We didn't care whether or not it was a boys' club either while we were building it. That's why it wasn't brought up. We voted when it was done. And the majority wanted boys."

"Pat wasn't there when you voted?" Mrs. Haley asked.

"No, I was slaving over lunch," Pat said bitterly.

"You see, we decided we wanted the whole

thing to be a secret organization with secret passwords and certain handshakes and different codes. Can you see girls keeping secrets like that? Soon all those giggly girls in Pat's grade would know them and spread them around, and that would spoil everything." Kurt paused and cleared his throat.

"I *can* keep a secret!" Pat almost shouted. Kurt shook his head.

"I hate to bring this up, Pat, but remember the time I had that boil on my rear end, and you said you wouldn't tell *anyone*? Before I got to class, *everyone* in the room knew about it and watched me when I sat down."

"I only told my best friend."

"You might as well have told it over the news on the biggest network. See, that's what I mean. Girls can't keep. . . ." Kurt stopped and looked at his mother. "I'm just talking about girls," he added.

"I certainly hope so," Mrs. Haley said sternly. "Also, I happen to know that Pat can keep a secret as well as anyone — when she wants to," she added.

"The whole thing comes down to the fact that the boys don't want girls around at the meetings — is that right?" Mr. Haley asked.

"I guess." Jeff looked doubtfully at Kurt.

Pat jumped up again. "But the boys have their friend, Sam."

"Sam furnished most of the nails and a lot of lumber from Granny's old barn. Besides, Sam's like family."

"Sam wanted to vote for Pat," Donnie reported then wilted when Kurt gave him a hard glare. "They only gave me half a vote," he added sadly.

Mr. Haley had a twinkle in his eyes, but his voice was stern. "Patricia, do you think you worked enough on the tree house to justify your occupying it with equal rights as the boys?"

Pat stood and squared her shoulders, tossing back her hair. "Yes I did. I'll bet I did more work than the four boys put together."

That brought a' big protest from all the boys.

"Speak one at a time, please. Do you honestly think that Patricia worked as hard as you boys on this project?"

The boys looked at each other and finally nodded.

"But her sandwiches were sloppy — all the insides in one big glob in the middle. You had to chew and chew on crusts before you got to anything." Donnie said.

"And she did say over and over that it was fun working on the tree house," Jeff accused.

"That's because I thought I'd be a member of the whatever-you-call-it club."

Mrs. Haley leaned over and whispered

something to the judge who nodded. But before Mr. Haley could open his mouth, Kurt began talking and because he was excited, his voice kept sliding up and down. The whole speech was almost funny. "Dad, you know when you were a boy how you wanted to be alone sometimes? If we let girls inside, the whole thing will be spoiled. They'll be wanting to do different things than . . ."

"Relax, Kurt, we're not going to force you to take in girls."

The boys gasped with relief, and Pat stared at her father in horror. She couldn't believe he'd let her down like that. But Mrs. Haley was smiling at her.

"We think that in all fairness Pat should be paid for all the work she put into *your* tree house."

All sorts of funny noises came from the divan where the boys sat.

"What do you think would be fair pay?" Mr. Haley asked Pat.

Pat sniffed and dug at a splinter in her thumb. "About fifty cents an hour."

Mr. Haley ignored the strangled noises the boys made.

"How many hours work do you think you put in?"

"About a hundred." Pat kept her eyes down.

"Hundred!" Kurt and Jeff were stunned, but Donnie looked at his sister admiringly.

"That would be almost a million dollars," he marveled.

"That's plain crazy!" Kurt roared. "What do you think we are, tycoons?"

"What's a tycoon?" Donnie didn't know for sure whether he wanted to be one or not.

"That's too high, Pat," Mrs. Haley said.

"I'll call Sam." Kurt left the room and was back in only a few minutes. "We decided to ask Pat to be a member of the Tree-Top-Tigers." He turned to glare at Pat. "You've got to promise not to go blabbing to anyone, you hear? Or *out* you go."

"On my ear, in a terrible snowstorm?" Pat asked sarcastically. "I don't really think I want to belong to that club of sneaky slobs. I think I'd rather have the money."

"How much do you want?" Jeff asked.

"Twenty dollars."

The groans from the divan sounded like several people were dying.

"That's too much," Mrs. Haley said again.

Mr. Haley got up. "Well, boys, I guess you fellows will have to work harder this summer. You won't have as much time for baseball, swimming, or fishing because you'll be too busy hiring out in town to cut lawns and earn that money."

Pat almost laughed out loud when she saw the looks on her brothers' faces. The idea of all that work was killing them.

Mrs. Haley looked stern. "You think this over, Pat. Maybe you could accept a little less money. You know your brothers have to work hard for what they earn."

"And so do I," Pat said proudly. "I'll give you my decision tomorrow." She stalked from the room.

Later, when she was in bed, her mother made the usual rounds of the bedrooms with the same words she said every night when she came in to kiss them goodnight. "Don't forget to say your prayers."

"Yes, I guess I'll say them. I wasn't going to but now I can." Pat snuggled down under the blankets.

Mrs. Haley paused, her hand on the lamp switch. "Why weren't you going to say your prayers, young lady?"

"Because I couldn't very well ask God to forgive me when as sure as heck I wasn't about to forgive the boys. . . . But now I guess I will."

"Pat, Pat, you know you would *have* to forgive them — even if you hadn't had your way. You couldn't go on every day carrying a grudge."

"Well, maybe."

"You think about that," Mrs. Haley said soberly. "It's easy to forgive when you come out on top." Mrs. Haley bent to kiss her, then turned out the light and left the room.

Pat did think about it. First, she didn't really think she was on top. Second, she really was still angry at the boys — all four of them. She wondered if you could say the Lord's Prayer and just leave out the forgiveness part. Maybe, if you just skipped it and kept on being mad at someone then God would take it for granted that you didn't expect to be forgiven either.

But Pat gave up that idea. She knew God would forgive her anyway. And then she didn't really like the idea of letting God think she wanted all her meanness to pile up and accumulate like the garbage and junk in some of the big cities she'd seen. Besides, all those parts of the prayer were fastened together something like a chain. If you took out one link, the whole thing would fall apart. All through the years all the good people had been saying that prayer over and over, and here was one crazy girl breaking up the whole thing.

She forgave the boys.

CHAPTER 3

The following day, which was Saturday, Pat decided to act as though all that unpleasantness hadn't happened. She felt very noble. She might get mad at them again sometime, but she'd keep a little extra forgiveness stored away inside her. But one thing she had to do. She had to have a talk with Sam.

The boys were eating a late breakfast, and her father had already gone in to work on some special project. Her mother was drinking a second cup of coffee and reading the morning paper. Pat said she was going up on the hill to look for the thermos jug. But instead of going directly up the hill, she walked down the road toward Granny's house. She knew Granny would be up early because Granny was by habit an early riser. Granny would also have gotten Sam up because the trim on the roof of her house needed painting.

The house was almost a hundred years old, and while it wasn't a big house at the time it was built, Granny said that it had been considered an elegant place. It was built of brick that time had faded to a beautiful pink, and the porch banisters and posts had been carved by a smart but lazy brother of Granny's. Granny had been born in the house.

Granny always fussed and complained about those fancy posts and banisters because she remembered so well how she had to do the hard fieldwork while her lazy brother sat in the shade and whittled on the posts. But that didn't keep her from having them painted every year. Secretly she was proud of them. Pat thought they were hideous, but she was very careful never to say it in front of Granny.

When she got to Granny's house, she met Sam coming out of the kitchen door. He was carrying a bucket of white paint and a brush and looked grumpy.

"Sam isn't exactly jumping with joy," Granny said, standing at the door with a big mug of coffee in her hand.

Pat looked at the fancy curlicues and flower petals that seemed to be thrown just any which way all over the posts and banisters. "It's funny that the wood has lasted so many years," she mused. "You'd think it would have rotted after all this time."

"I've invited every termite for miles around to come feast on it, but not one has ever accepted. We keep the darn stuff too well painted." Sam began to stir the big bucket of white paint.

"It took my brother Hugo six months to

do that carving. He started in spring and worked on it until the weather got cold."

"Smart Hugo," Sam muttered, but Granny didn't hear him because she had gone to the other side of the porch.

"Some of his pictures are so pretty. Come look at this one. He said it was the face of an angel, and he copied my face. I'll never forget that day. We were haying, and it was the hottest day that summer, but when I saw how he carved his little sister's face in the wood, I forgot all about my misery."

Pat went over to look at the carving, but she couldn't see anything that looked like a face. There was something that resembled a nose but nothing more.

"You think it looks like Granny?" Sam asked. The crinkles were at his eyes, but his smile didn't spread.

"Well," Pat said slowly, "I don't know what Granny looked like when she was a little girl, but I'm sure that if Hugo said it looked like Granny . . ." Her voice trailed off because Sam was watching her with those cool eyes that had laughter behind them, and she was afraid she would smile too.

"Oh, he said it all right. He was the laziest tramp on earth, but at least he was a truthful one. I'm sure he carved my face."

They saw the mail car stop by the box,

and Granny ran out to talk to Mr. Head. This was the chance Pat wanted.

"Sam, did you really vote against having me in the tree house club?"

Sam's eyes widened in surprise. "I don't get it. Last night Kurt called me like he was on the hot line, and he was considering setting off the bomb. And what was it? Whether or not you were to be allowed in the club."

"Well?"

"Well?" Sam mocked her.

"I thought the whole thing was to be one big joke, but my brothers didn't. They really *didn't* want me in that club."

"It wasn't even a club yet. Oh, Pat, you got yourself all worked up over nothing! Of course, when the boys saw how mad you were, they went right along with it. I know they give you a bad time once in a while, but why don't you *laugh*? You'll find out they'll leave you alone then."

"Maybe you thought it was all a joke, but my brothers did *not*. They really didn't want me in that club."

"I told you it wasn't a club yet," Sam said gently, the faraway look in his blue eyes kept telling Pat that as far as he was concerned the subject was closed.

Granny came up then, a puzzled frown on

34

her face as she watched the old mail car go down the road.

"I'll never understand Mr. Head." She took a sip of coffee from the big brown mug. "He gets a little nuttier every day."

Sam finished stirring the paint and went over to the other end of the porch. He did not look at Pat again but as he put a dab of paint on the bulge that was supposed to be a copy of Granny's face, Pat saw the smile crinkles around his eyes.

"What did Mr. Head do now?" Pat wasn't really too interested in Mr. Head's nutty tendencies, but she knew Granny wanted to talk about it.

"Ghosts!" Granny said dramatically.

"Did he see one?" Pat asked.

Granny sat down on the porch steps and drank her coffee. "You know that old, broken-down rock house near the river? My Grandpa and Grandma built it themselves out of the rocks from right around here. It was before the Civil War, and for a while they used it for a hospital. I hated to have it torn down. It's not bothering anyone that far back from the road."

"And now Mr. Head saw a ghost in the house, and he's afraid it will be getting mail, and Mr. Head will have to deliv . . ."

"Sam, you get to your painting! Look at

that river of paint running down your arm and onto your jeans."

Pat tried not to smile. "Go on with your story, Granny. What makes Mr. Head think there are ghosts in that old house?"

"He said that twice when he drove home after bowling he saw a light flickering in the back of the house. There were two rooms added to it right about the time this house was built. Hugo wanted to live in it. Well, anyway, those two rooms still have a roof and part of a window pane, and that's where Mr. Head saw the light."

"Mr. Head drinks too many beers when he bowls. He admits it. He told me so himself. Whenever their team wins, they have a round of beers," Sam contributed from the other side of the porch.

"But he saw lights twice in one week." Granny poured out the rest of her coffee. "And last night he went to prayer meeting, and he saw a light again — not a steady light, but a flickering one. Now, they don't serve beer at a prayer meeting." Granny's voice was severe.

"Granny, you told me lots of times that you had to take everything Mr. Head says with a bucket of salt."

Granny nodded. "You're right, child. Where are you going so early?"

"Up on the hill to see if I can find that thermos jug I dumped there yesterday."

"Keep your eyes on the ground, and if you see any mushrooms, we'll all go mushroom hunting this afternoon."

As she walked up the hill, Pat thought some more about what Sam had told her about the tree house. She did remember how softly he had "read" the constitution. Had there been laughter behind that make-believe reading? And when had the joke turned serious? Because she knew the boys at the court session had been dead serious. She'd ask Donnie; he'd tell her.

She reached the top of the hill and went over to the mulberry tree. There, as big and plain as a candidate's signboard, stood the thermos jug. There was no sign of a paper sack, but the jug was there. It was *not* there yesterday when she went back to look for it. She picked it up and opened it. There wasn't even a smell of lemonade. Someone had rinsed it out. It *had* to be one of the boys, and these jokes were going too far. All forgiveness forgotten, she began to get angry again.

She started down the hill but stopped when she heard a rustle in the bushes beside the path. Although she had not taken Poochie with her, often he went looking for her on his own. She called but Poochie did not come out. Pat started to look for him in the bushes but then remembered that only last week they had seen a copperhead on the rocks not too far away.

It had made them all very cautious. So she abandoned her search and went on home. Funny things were happening. It didn't seem much of a joke to refuse a sister membership in a club. Nor was it funny to hide a thermos jug, then return it all empty and clean.

And regardless of Mr. Head and his beers, Pat didn't think that caused him to see lights in the old, broken-down house. That wasn't funny either. She really didn't think the boys were doing all those things. They certainly couldn't be roaming out in the woods at ten o'clock at night — not with a mother that made the rounds of the bedrooms. No, there was something else happening, and Pat was going to find out what it was.

When she got back to their yard, she saw Donnie raking dead leaves from the bushes and hedges.

"It was there after all?" He asked, looking at the thermos jug.

"Did *you* put it back? Because it definitely was not there yesterday."

"No, I didn't," Donnie said indignantly. "You were just too mad about the tree house club to really look for that jug."

Pat set the jug down. "Donnie, look at me and tell me the truth." Her voice was serious.

"I *am*! I haven't seen that jug until just this minute. You just didn't look very good."

"No," Pat broke in, "that's not what I'm talking about. I believe you about the jug. What I want to know is when you guys painted that sign about not having any girls, were you just playing a joke on me?"

Donnie's eyes widened behind the glasses that somehow looked too big on his little face. "How did you find out?"

"Never mind. Just tell me this. When did it all turn into being serious and mad? I *know* the boys did not want me in that club."

"It was just a joke at first," Donnie said slowly, frowning as he tried to remember. "But when you got so awfully mad and ran off with the lunch, the boys got mad too."

"What boys?"

"Oh, Jeff and Kurt. Kurt mostly. Did you ever notice how Kurt is always the first to get mad?"

"And Sam?"

"Sam thought it was a joke when he left. He had to go home and help Granny with something. He left soon after you ran to the woods."

Pat said nothing, thinking hard.

"Anyway, we didn't have a constitution or a secret handshake or anything like that, although I think it would be lots of fun."

Pat looked around. "By the way, where's Poochie?"

Donnie looked sad. "I don't know what's

come over my dog. He doesn't love me anymore. The only time he shows up is late afternoon when it's feeding time. Where do you suppose he hangs out all day? He always liked me before."

"I don't know," Pat frowned. Another bit of a puzzle that didn't really fit anywhere, unless, of course, dogs and ghosts and thermos jugs somehow got together.

"You do put him in his pen every night, don't you?"

"Oh, yes, he's safe in his pen 'cause a fox might get him otherwise."

"I don't really think there are any foxes around these woods," Pat said.

"That's where you're wrong." Kurt came around the corner of the house. "Sam and I saw a good-sized fox in the woods last week. Today Granny called up Mom and said she wouldn't have any eggs to sell Mom this week because something had gotten in the nests every night and taken the eggs. Granny thought it might be a fox."

"A fox!" Donnie exclaimed in horror. "Do they eat people . . . or dogs?"

"Of course not," Kurt said in what Pat called his superior way. "Foxes, unless they are starving, wouldn't attack even a white-livered pup like Poochie."

"You worry about your own liver!" Donnie

cried angrily. "I'll bet it gets white sometimes too."

Someone laughed and Sam came right behind Kurt.

"I think all of us get white-livered sometimes, if you mean by that that we get scared," he said. "I've seen you scared, Kurt, and you've certainly seen me the same way."

Kurt never got angry when Sam said things like that but if Jeff or Pat had said it, he would have been furious.

"I know what really happened," Jeff said as he turned the corner. "Poochie thinks he's really a fox, and he joined the foxes' club, see? Well, he became very popular, and they asked him to run for president. He said he would, and he's been out electioneering all day. That's why you haven't seen him. But soon they'll begin looking into his background (like they do to all the candidates), and they'll find out he's just a dog and make him go back to being a dog again."

"You know, kid, you're going to be the writer of the family," Kurt snickered. "Now, isn't that a great story, Donnie?"

"No, it's not!" Donnie snapped. "If Poochie got kicked out of a club just because he's a dog, it would hurt his feelings. I don't want him to be hurt in his feelings."

"And it *does* hurt your feelings! Believe me, *I* know," Pat said loudly and flounced into the house.

CHAPTER 4

The little bits of puzzle floated around in Pat's mind but did not quite fit anywhere. Were there really foxes around that raided Granny's henhouse every evening? Maybe the lights in the old house were true and someone was stealing things. Or, was it all tied in with the big joke the boys were playing on her? There had not been one single tree house meeting that Pat knew of. The house nestled in the green leaves.

Saturday afternoon Granny called up and said she had found some big mushrooms in the orchard and that it might be a good time to look for them in the bottoms near the river. The older boys had a baseball game at the field three miles away, and Mom had taken Donnie to the dentist. So that left only Pat to go with Granny. Much later Pat learned that Granny knew everyone else's plans and had wanted only Pat to go along with her.

Pat loved being with Granny. She saw so many new spring things that Pat would certainly have missed by herself. And it was a beautiful day. The redbud laced the woods with color, and every tree seemed to be a choir loft full of singing birds. Granny plodded on until they came in sight of the old, broken-down rock house.

"Indians lived around here when my Grandpa built this place," she said. "Maybe even some Indians helped him." Her eyes had a faraway look.

"Most of the stories show the Indians and whites fighting," Pat observed.

"Well, from what I remember of Grandpa's stories (and he was always the one who talked), he and the Indians were good to each other and helped out when things got bad."

"I don't see one single mushroom," said Pat.

"Mushrooms never grow here." Granny's eyes were studying the ground.

"Then why on earth did we come down here?"

Granny pointed to a path that led from the woods to the old rock house. It wasn't a hard-beaten path, but it had definitely been used a lot lately because the grass and weeds were pressed down.

"Poochie could have made that path all by himself," she said. "He must come down here every day." She turned to look at the two back rooms that had been added to the old house. "Hello, anyone home?" she called.

It gave Pat an eerie feeling. She expected

to see some odd head pop out of the back door.

"Where is Poochie today?" Granny asked, keeping her eyes on the back door.

"We tied him up in his pen. Donnie's afraid he might join the Fox Club that has been raiding your henhouse."

"A mighty funny pack of foxes. They seem to wear plastic hair pins. I found a pink one yesterday. And that's not all — three of the eggs had been returned. They were all in one nest. Now, wouldn't you say that's no club for Poochie to be running around with?"

Pat was dumbfounded. "You don't think the boys are playing these tricks on us, do you?"

"Not for one minute. Sam's been busy painting, and you've got the kind of mother who keeps track of her kids too. That's why I wanted to come down here. It could just be that some transient family is camping out here for a while. Now, I don't mind one bit, and I'll even give them food and clothes, if they need it, but I *won't* have them stealing."

Granny started down the path to the back of the house.

"Where are you going, Granny?" Pat cried. "Please don't go in! You don't know who might be living there — they could be murderers."

"Then I think I'd better find out, don't you?"

"But how can you if you're murdered?" At the time Pat didn't think the conversation was one bit funny but much later she and Granny had a good laugh over it.

Although she had a wild desire to tear up the path to their own safe territory, the sight of tiny little Granny marching to the back of the house made her ashamed, and she ran to catch up. The door stood open about an inch and Granny knocked sharply.

"Even if this is my house, nonpaying tenants have some rights."

There was no sound from the inside, and Granny pushed the door wide. The first glance convinced both of them that someone was living there. The place was filthy, but someone had made an effort to get rid of the spiders and animal nests. There was a pot of water next to the remains of an open fire on the dirt floor in the front room where there was no roof. The water was still warm. There was a rope with blankets hanging on it stretched across the two rooms, and on a table sat some paper plates and cups and two or three candles.

"Mr. Head did see lights," said Pat, holding up a candle stub stuck on a bit of tin.

Granny shook her head sadly. "Who would have to live in a wreck like this? And I know a lady who said to me the other day that we had no really *poor* people in our town. She

said poor people only lived in big cities."

"I wonder who and what they are? I don't see any signs of clothes or food." Pat started to open the drawers of the old cabinet, but Granny shook her head.

"No, let's not. They have a right to their own business. How would you like strangers going through your belongings?"

"I'd hate it, but our house *is* our house, and no one has a right to poke around in it."

Granny's face looked very grave. She waited until Pat had gone out the door, then she carefully closed it to the same position it had been in when they got there.

"Pat, I have a feeling someone here could use our help."

"Well then, why don't we just hang around and offer whoever turns up some food and stuff?"

Granny walked briskly down the path as though she was afraid they would run into someone. "If these people wanted to ask for help they could go to the Welfare Agency or the Salvation Army in town. Whoever they are, they don't want to ask for help. People can be very proud, you know."

"But not too proud to steal food."

"Let's try to find out more about them before we say that to *anyone*." Granny looked sternly at Pat. "Maybe we can help them without making a big deal about it."

"I won't tell anyone. I can keep a secret," Pat said crossly. "But remember there's someone else who thinks something's going on here, and he isn't exactly the kind of person who would shut up about it."

"You mean Mr. Head?"

"Yes. If he told you, maybe he told every other woman on his route."

"I think the reason Mr. Head told me is because I own the place. He might have felt I had a right to know if something funny was going on there."

"Well, something funny *is* going on, that's for sure." Pat felt uneasy walking through the woods. She had the feeling someone was watching her, and once when a squirrel jumped from one limb to another above them, she jumped too and screamed.

"What did you think it was, a bunch of apes?" Granny sounded a little disgusted. "Let's cut through the woods to the road. It's about time for Mr. Head to come along, and I'd like to ask him a few questions."

Pat followed her happily.

They just made it in time. Mr. Head was bumping slowly down the road, sitting on the opposite side of the seat from the steering wheel as usual so he could drop the mail in the box. He stopped when he saw them and looked uneasily at Granny's empty basket.

"No mushrooms?" he asked nervously. "You should go up on the hill beyond your orchard. If the mushrooms are out at all, you'll find them there."

"I really wasn't too serious about finding mushrooms," replied Granny. "There's something else on my mind."

Mr. Head fiddled with a pack of letters.

"Have you seen any more lights at the old homestead?" asked Granny.

He looked straight ahead. "I haven't seen any more lights. I don't think I saw any last week either. . . . You know how it is. . . ." He gave a sickly laugh. "You get a few beers in you, and you begin to imagine things."

"No, I don't know how it is, never having had a few beers in me, Mr. Head," Granny said reproachfully. "Now, you told me you saw lights on the night when you went to prayer meeting too."

"I guess it was just a reflection of my own headlights on a window. I know now there were no lights." He raced his motor. "Guess I'd better move on. I'm running late this afternoon."

They watched the car go over the crest of the hill.

"That old coot knows something, and now all of a sudden he won't tell," Granny snapped.

"So, now what do we do? I don't think

either one of us can sleep knowing someone is just barely living in that rat's nest down there. Why, Granny, what's to keep a fox out of there?"

"They can keep big animals out," she said thoughtfully. "Common sense tells me to mind my own business. If someone needed help, they know where to go in the town, and they'd get it too. Now, that's what common sense tells me, and, still, I'm like you, Pat. I won't be able to sleep tonight. I'll have to do some very serious thinking." They walked in silence for a while, then Granny spoke again.

"Pat, you're right. Some kids might be temporarily camping there, and they sure don't want a nosy old woman and a kid barging in with a loaf of bread and a link of sausage. That would explain Mr. Head's backing out of the mystery. And Poochie could just be enjoying some new company."

Pat shook her head.

"You said I'm right, but I didn't say a thing. I do think you're right, though, and we'd better lay low before we do anything. What about the nervous way Mr. Head acted just now?"

"Oh, Mr. Head's funny. Any man who stays a bachelor for fifty-five years without a woman to keep him sane is going to act peculiar now and then. Come on, child. Let's go to the orchard and hunt for mushrooms."

CHAPTER 5

Granny refused to talk about the old house anymore, and since Mr. Head always had the mail delivered before the children got home from school, Pat didn't get to ask him anything. Granny's eggs appeared neatly in the right nest, for the right hens, and Poochie lived a sad life tied up in his pen until Donnie came home from school. So suddenly all the funny little bits of mystery seemed to mean nothing to anyone except Pat. Curiosity urged her to go back to the old house, but she was afraid to go alone. Besides, there were always things that she had to do when she came home from school.

Saturday, too, was a busy day because the grass was beginning to grow, and the hedges needed to be trimmed. Mom's flower beds were filled with last year's dead leaves, and already weeds were pushing their sassy little heads out of the ground. Sam didn't come down because he was still painting faces that didn't look like faces and flowers that didn't look like flowers.

Then a funny, important thing happened. Mrs. Haley was going to take all three boys to town to buy them new Sunday shoes when at the last minute Donnie couldn't find his red tennis shoes. He tearfully maintained that he'd left them under the big oak by the tree house. Immediately it went through Pat's mind that probably the thermos-egg gremlin was at work again. When no one could find the tennis shoes, Mrs. Haley told Donnie to wear his old Sunday shoes and off they went.

It was a hot muggy day and tremendous white clouds were piling higher and higher in the sky. For a while Pat enjoyed just sitting and watching them because they changed shapes so rapidly they seemed like one of those new movies that flash a new scene at you before you can really see what the one before is. But even cloud-watching got boring, and Pat realized that being home alone was no fun. It would have been better to go to the shoestore and watch three boys try on shoes. She decided to let Poochie out of his pen, hike with him to the river, and wade in the shallows to cool off.

Not a breath of air stirred, and all around one got a kind of uneasy feeling that always comes before a big storm. Pat stayed on the path, but Poochie tore ahead of her toward the rock house. Watching him, there was no doubt in her mind that this was a very welcome place for the dog. Finally, she admitted to herself that she'd intended going here all along.

The path to the back of the old house was much more worn than it had been when she and Granny had been there before. When she got to the door, she saw a pair of small red tennis shoes on the threshold. They were marked with the big "D" that Donnie had printed on right after he got them.

Poochie rushed around the house barking joyfully and Pat followed him. Spread in the shade of a big oak was a quilt and on top of it, just stirring from sleep, was a little girl about Donnie's size. In a second the child was up and running like a wild creature into the woods. Poochie, thinking it was a game, was right beside her. Pat broke into the chase without half thinking. But fast as she was, she knew she would never overtake the small flying figure. Then Poochie in his eagerness to keep up with the little girl got twisted between her legs and she fell. She sprang up in a flash but by that time Pat was up with her and grabbed her wrist. Dark blue eyes, almost black with rage, blazed at Pat.

"You let me go. You let me go right now!" She ground the words through small white teeth that looked ready to bite.

Pat tightened her grasp as the child twisted and squirmed like an eel.

"I'm not going to hurt you. Why should I? I just want to talk to you."

"I'm not going to talk to *you*. I'm not supposed to talk to anyone. It's your dumb dog that

showed you where we live. We didn't hurt anything. We even cleaned it up a little. You can't
call the police — we didn't do anything."

"Listen to me. Why should I call the
police? Don't be silly. I'm tickled to have you
here. I only have brothers, and I've always
wanted a girl around. Do please sit down and
talk to me. What's your name?"

"Bloom."

"Bloom?"

"Isn't that the craziest name you ever
heard? Su . . . I mean, *somebody* told me they
named me that because the flowers were bloom-
ing." She watched Pat suspiciously while she
talked. Pat led her gently back to the house but
did not loosen her grip on the little wrist.

"I think it's pretty. My name is Pat, and
I don't know why I was called that." Out of the
corner of her eye she could see Bloom trying to
kick the red tennis shoes out of sight.

Pat sat down on the door sill and pulled
the little girl down beside her. "Who lives here
with you?"

"I'm not supposed to talk, I told you."
Bloom tried to pull her wrist away, but Pat
held on.

Pat glanced over her shoulder into the
two rooms. "I'll bet it rains in that broken roof,
doesn't it?"

"It hasn't rained since we came here, and soon we'll be gone, and then we won't care."

"Let me guess how old you are."

"I won't tell you anyway. I'm not supposed to talk to anyone. How many times do I have to *tell* you?" she lashed out furiously.

Pat refused to get angry. "I have a little brother about your size. He's in the first grade and is beginning to read. I'll bet you know a few words too."

"It's none of your business." The dark eyes were sullen.

Pat got up and released the child. "I am really sorry. I *did* want to have a girl for a friend, but I can see you don't like me so I might as well take my dog and go home." She turned to go.

"Wait! Are you going to tell the cops about us living here?" The eyes were no longer sullen; they were afraid.

"Of course not. I know the lady that owns the place. We call her Granny. And she certainly doesn't care if you camp here for a while."

Bloom's face lighted and for the first time looked pretty. She stooped and picked up the tennis shoes. "I'm sorry I took them, but I needed them and Sue had to save her money for . . . for something else. I took other things too. We ate the sandwiches because you threw them away anyhow, and we figured we were as important as a rabbit or squirrel. We put the jug back."

"Did you have eggs for breakfast?" Pat asked cooly.

Bloom's eyes narrowed. "No, Sue told me to take them back. But I fell and broke some so I only had three left. Were those the old lady's eggs?"

"She didn't mind. But after this, if there's anything you need you just ask us. We'll be glad to help you out. That's what neighbors do in the country."

Bloom was silent for a moment. Then she said, "That sounds nice, but Sue won't let me ask anybody for anything."

"Is Sue your mother?"

"No, Sue's my sister. My mother ran away."

"Why don't you keep these tennis shoes? My mother will probably buy my brother some more this afternoon."

Bloom backed away. "No, Sue would be mad at me. But thank you," she added hastily. "And I do like you. I think you're nice, unless you're lying. Lots and lots of people lie. I . . . I try not to believe anyone."

"Please believe me, Bloom. Oh, I guess I lie sometimes too, but I try not to and I'm *not* lying to you. I'd like to be your friend."

Just then a crash of thunder shook the

earth, and Pat saw that the gorgeous castle-white clouds had turned gray-black with snakes of lightning in them. She glanced in the kitchen. Only one small corner was covered with a roof. If the wind blew in the half-broken window anyone inside would be drenched.

"Where's your sister now?" she asked.

"She's at work. She works at the dime store. She rides home with the mailman at five o'clock."

"And there's no one around to take care of you?"

"I can take care of myself—I'm over six. . . ." She clapped her hand over her mouth as if she realized she'd given something away.

"I think you'd better come home with me, Bloom. It's going to storm, and this is no place to be when it rains. I'll bring you back before your sister comes home so she won't worry."

They couldn't yet feel the wind in the valley, but it had begun to moan up in the tree tops. Another crash of thunder shattered the air. Poochie gave a terrified yipe and ran for home. Pat put her arms around the little girl. "Honey, please listen to me. I *am not lying.* It's going to storm, and I'll bet your sister would be glad to know you were safe and dry. Maybe I could call her at the store and tell her."

"You can't call her at the store unless

you're dead. They have rules," Bloom said flatly. "I want to be here when she comes home. You go ahead. I'm not afraid. I'll crawl under the table, and if I get wet that won't hurt me. You'd better go right now."

The wind was no longer a sighing moan. It was a frightening roar and getting louder every second. The darkness was frightening too, and the thunder crashed and rolled without stopping.

"What a kid!" Pat thought. "She couldn't be much more than six, and here she is alone and willing to sit out a storm in a broken-down house all by herself."

Pat pushed her into the back room and shoved the small table against the wall. "Run out and get that quilt and hurry," she ordered. She herself dragged some old boards from a corner and piled them on the table, which seemed sturdy enough to hold up an elephant.

Bloom came in with the quilt, and Pat grabbed another one off the line. Outside the first big drops of rain were falling, driven by the wind.

"Under the table!" Pat ordered and crawled under it too. Bloom showed no sign of fear. "What kind of a life did this kid have?" Pat wondered, already beginning to love the quiet little girl who was too loyal to her sister to go to safe shelter.

There was another deafening crash of thunder, and then the rain really came. The girls wrapped themselves in the quilts and huddled close together. The noise of the storm was horrible, and it was impossible to talk. Pat put her arms around Bloom and wrapped the quilts more tightly around the both of them. Water inched across the floor and they were soon soaked. One time Bloom lifted a corner of the dripping quilt from Pat's face and without a word smiled into her eyes. For one brief second Pat was so warmed and thrilled by that look that she forgot all about the fearful storm and how worried her family must be.

But then a huge rock in the wall, loosened by the driving rain, gave way and crashed — almost at their feet. Pat screamed and even Bloom jumped. After that Pat was really frightened. A second rock could fall right on them. "Please, God, help us," she said out loud.

Bloom lifted the blanket again and stared at her.

"What did you say?" she yelled in Pat's ear.

"I'm praying."

"Praying?"

"Yes, to God. I'm scared." Pat looked straight into Bloom's dark eyes. "You'd better pray too."

"I don't know anything about God."

61

Pat said nothing. She just shivered and held the little girl closer to her, trying to pull further away from the crumbling rock. But in her mind she was still praying. The sound of the wind was lessening, and the lightning and thunder seemed more distant, but the rain still came in torrents and little bits of rock continued to wash off with the water pouring over the wall.

"Yes, I do." Bloom's mouth was so close to Pat's ear that she could feel the warm breath.

"What?"

"I know something about God. You want me to sing it?"

Pat couldn't believe she heard correctly, but she nodded anyway. Then, in a half whisper, Bloom sang in her ear. "God Bless America." She knew the whole song, and as she finished she looked at Pat expectantly.

"Beautiful," Pat said and Bloom didn't know that tears were mixed with the rain on her face. Somehow that song was one of the most beautiful pieces of music she'd ever heard.

She had no idea how much time had passed but at last she caught a glimpse of flashlights and lanterns and heard her father's voice call out, "You there, Pat?"

Sam and Kurt were with him. Kurt had brought Pat's raincoat and threw it around her. Sam cuddled Bloom under his big yellow coat, which she permitted doubtfully, keeping a tight hold on Pat's hand.

"Nice weather we're having!" Sam said with his smile all out and all for Bloom. Even Bloom couldn't resist that smile.

"Who's your friend?" Kurt asked, smiling at the little girl but getting no smile in return.

"Dad, how did you know I was here?" Pat asked as they sloshed through the mud and grass toward the road where the car was parked.

"Mr. Head."

"Mr. Head?"

"Let's get in the car and I can explain later. We'll drop you at home and then take your little friend to Granny's." The two girls crowded in the front seat with Mr. Haley.

"It's like this. It seems that Mr. Head has been taking this young girl to work in town each morning and bringing her home each evening. You know it's over a three-mile walk."

Pat nodded. "Bloom told me. It's her sister."

"Well, this evening we had three inches of rain in an hour's time, and the creek was so high no cars could go through. The girl was worried about her little sister, who seemed to be living somewhere around here, and so Mr. Head called Granny. I didn't even know Granny had a house she rented out."

"She hasn't. These two girls live, or camp,

in that old deserted homestead that's falling to bits."

"I can't believe it!" Mr. Haley said, and even the boys in the back seat gasped in disbelief.

"Well, anyway, Mr. Head called Granny, but by that time the storm was on in full force. Granny called us, and Mother told her you were gone so we all figured you must have come up here and found the child."

"I'm not a child." Evidently Bloom didn't like all the conversation about Sue and her. Her eyes were sullen and angry.

"He calls everyone under fifty a child— don't let that bother you," Kurt said from the back seat.

"So, we'll drop you off at home, Pat, and take your friend to Granny's where Mr. Head will drop Sue as soon as the creek goes down a little more."

"Please, please, stay with me," Bloom pleaded, holding on to Pat.

"Dad, don't drop me off at home. You can explain to Mom when you get back. I'm the only one Bloom knows, and I'd like to stay with her until her sister gets there. Granny won't mind having me, will she, Sam?"

"Gosh, no. You can have my bedroom, and I'll sleep on the couch in the TV room."

"You can come home with us, Sam," Kurt suggested. "You can sleep in Pat's room."

Mr. Haley agreed to this plan, and Bloom sighed in relief.

CHAPTER 6

Granny was good at just about anything, but when it came to dragging in two soaked girls, giving them hot baths, feeding them, and tucking them into beds already warmed by electric blankets, she was absolutely tops. Bloom and Pat giggled when they saw each other in Granny's long-sleeved flannel nightgowns. Pat looked lost, but Bloom was almost invisible.

"I like this," she said wrapping the gown around her legs. "It's clean and it's warm and that's more than Sue and I have had for a week."

After a shy little smile she added, "I like you too, Pat, I really do. You're not one of the lying kind." She cuddled deep under the blankets. "And when you feel like it, you can teach me another song or speech with God in it. They give me a nice feeling."

"You know why?" Pat rolled up the sleeves of the nightgown.

"No, why?"

"Because God is Someone who really never lies."

"Then I got to know Him, I never . . ." Bloom's voice got slower and slower till Pat knew she had finally fallen asleep. As Pat turned to look at her, she felt the same warm tenderness she used to feel when Donnie was still so little and helpless.

Pat herself was much too excited to sleep, and when she heard the front door open and Granny talking, she got up, slipped on one of Granny's flowered housecoats, and tiptoed out to see who it was.

A small, thin girl, who looked a lot like Bloom without her childish softness, stood just inside the door. She was almost as wet as Pat and Bloom had been, and her face looked much too old and strained for such a young person.

"Is my sister all right?" she was asking Granny.

"She's sound asleep. She had food and a hot bath and is now in a warm bed. And, my child, that's exactly the treatment you're going to get too. What is your name?"

"Susan. Susan Spring. And I can't thank you enough for taking care of my little sister." Her chin quivered.

"You thank Pat Haley for that. Pat stayed with your sister all through the storm, and then Pat's dad brought them here."

Pat spoke up. "Bloom wasn't scared at all. She wasn't nearly as frightened as I was."

Sue turned to Granny. "I hope you didn't mind us using your house. We really didn't hurt anything, and we had no money to go to a motel."

Granny ignored this. "You take a warm bath, Susan Spring. I've put out some dry things for you."

"But, your house . . ." Sue began.

"After you're warm and dry," Granny continued, "come in the kitchen. Then you can tell us as much or as little as you like."

All that time Mr. Head had been standing at the door, his wet clothes dripping on Granny's clean rag rug.

"Thanks a lot, Mr. Head," Sue said as Pat led her off to the bathroom. The moment they were out of earshot Granny narrowed her eyes.

"Well, Mr. Head, what's all this about? You told me just two days ago that you were sure no one was living in that old house. You blamed your seeing those lights on too many beers. And now I hear you've been hauling that poor child back and forth to her work. Why so secret? We might have been able to help her too, you know."

Mr. Head shrugged.

"I saw her walking a couple of mornings and offered her a ride. No one else seems to go in that early from this part of the country. I said I might as well bring her home too, since she had to be on her feet all day."

"Why didn't you tell us that?"

Mr. Head's ears turned crimson.

"Because, with me being a single man and her being a single girl, I thought people might hear about it and think we were going to get married."

Granny's jaw dropped and she sank into her rocking chair. "Mr. Head, you are fifty-three years old, and this girl is barely sixteen! Have you flipped completely?"

He shuffled uneasily. "Lots of young girls like older men."

"That much older? You'd better go home, Mr. Head. You're ruining my rug *and* my regard. Goodnight."

No sooner had Mr. Head driven off than Granny got a pile of paper towels and tried to mop up the rain pools. She was laughing so hard that finally the two girls came in to find out what was going on.

The three of them sat around the kitchen table later, gorging themselves on hot chocolate and chicken-salad sandwiches.

"First really good food I've had since we left Dallas." Sue's face was relaxed and much better looking than Pat had first thought. She finished two sandwiches and two pieces of Granny's famous coffee cake.

"I haven't had a thing to eat all day. I saved my lunch money to take a treat to Bloom this evening. She loves hot dogs." Sue stirred

70

her cocoa, then looked up. "I'd like to tell you how we got into this mess. You've been so good to us, I can't bear to have you think we're just plain starving trash."

"We know that," Granny said. "You don't have to tell us anything."

"I want to. You see Bloom is only my half sister. Her mother ran away right after Bloom was born. My mother had died and so there was only my dad and Bloom and me. Mostly I took care of her — although at that time Dad helped some too. But . . ." She gulped. "But he wasn't too well so by the time I was fifteen I practically took care of Bloom by myself. It was all right as long as Dad could watch her while I was at school, but sometimes he would forget or . . . well . . . he'd go out with the men, and Bloom just ran around like a little wild thing."

"How old are you, Sue?" Granny asked gently.

"I'm older than I look. I'm almost twenty. But I was scared to death they'd take Bloom away from me and . . . well . . . she's like my own child."

"I know she must be," Granny agreed.

"So I wrote my aunt and uncle in St. Louis and told them I could work and pay for Bloom and my way if only they would adopt us so that we could be together. They have no children, so they would be glad to have us. Dad was glad too that we would be in a real home, so he gave me the car and fifty dollars, and we started for St. Louis."

"That's quite a trip," Granny commented.

"Fifty dollars seemed like a lot of money at first, but things kept going wrong with the car, and I had to have them fixed. We ate only two meals a day, but even at that the money was soon gone. Then when we got here the transmission went out. We looked for a place to live and saw the old house and moved in. I got a job at the dime store so we could eat and I could save up to have the car fixed. I could have written to my uncle or aunt, but I hated to start out in a new family by asking for money. That first night we had nothing to eat, and so we took Pat's sandwiches. I didn't think that was too bad because she seemed to have thrown them away. They were very good." She smiled at Pat.

"They were horrible, but I'm glad you got them and the lemonade too, although that jug reappearing under the tree sort of puzzled me."

"Well, anyway, now I only have a week more to work, and then we'll have enough to pay for the car repair and go to our family."

"Don't you think we should call your aunt and uncle and tell them why it's taking you so long to get there?" Granny suggested. "They must be very worried."

So early the next morning Sue called her

relatives, and they insisted on driving down that same day to get the girls.

"They were horrified at what happened," Sue announced with delight.

Pat was disappointed in a way. She wanted to get to know the girls better.

"Maybe I can come back and visit when school's out," Bloom said consolingly. "By then I'll have learned a lot of new songs. My Aunt Lucia goes to church, Sue says, and they always sing songs with God in them. I'll learn three or four to sing to you."

The girls' aunt and uncle arrived without mishap a few hours later and hugged Bloom and Sue before they said a word to anyone else. Granny said later that she approved of them and was sure the girls would finally have a real home. But Pat cried when the car drove out of sight.

Kurt, who'd come over to check up on things, snorted impatiently.

"What are you bawling about? You only knew them for a few hours."

"But those were important hours," Granny said reprovingly. "Now behave yourself, boy, and I'll make you some of your favorite cookies."

"When was the last time I told you that

you were a good kid?" Kurt asked, squeezing her shoulder.

Granny chuckled. "You know very well that it was the 18th of January, 1896."

CHAPTER 7

It was the reading hour, and the four Haley children each had a book, although Donnie was mostly looking at pictures. He did know some words though, and occasionally he'd shout them out in delight which made the others furious. The Haley parents had started this reading hour some months ago when some of the teachers said that most children were watching too much TV, and, as a result, their reading ability was suffering.

"And who wants a 'suffering ability?'" Kurt laughed as he picked up his outdoor magazine.

Pat loved reading and was already deep in a book she'd gotten from the library. Jeff read, but unless he had a mystery, he got bored quickly and just sat daydreaming and turning pages. He thought he could write better stories than most of those he picked up at the library.

Tonight Donnie kept running back and forth from the kitchen to the recreation room. He'd decided to be a reporter of the family news.

"I think Mom's going to make fudge," he announced in a loud whisper. "She's getting out sugar and chocolate and milk and butter."

Then he sat down, opened his book, and tried to sound out a word he didn't know.

"Will you please shut up!" Kurt snapped. "You're not supposed to sound your words out loud anyway."

"How can you tell what they sound like then? I don't have ears inside my head," Donnie complained.

Jeff looked up and laughed. "You just keep your ears on the outside for decoration?"

"I'm trying to read," Pat reminded them. "And it's very selfish of you all to keep yakking all the time."

Donnie looked hurt and returned to the kitchen. In a moment he was back.

"Yes, she is! She's cooking fudge!" No one answered him, so he sat down and picked up his reader again.

Pat wasn't reading anymore. She was thinking of what the teacher had said to her at noon when she'd gotten mad because the other kids didn't want to play her game. The teacher had said it loud enough so that *everyone* could hear it. "You are being selfish, Patricia Haley."

That had hurt!

Pat knew well enough that she, of all people, was not selfish. How could one girl in a family of three boys have a chance to be selfish? If only her teacher had known what Pat had to put up with at home. Oh, yes, they always voted on what to do or play but the boys always stuck together because they didn't want to play *anything* that even smacked of a girl's game. Not that Pat didn't love boys' games. She did, but . . .

Donnie bounced in and out of the kitchen again.

"Smell it?" he asked.

The good, sweet, chocolate smell drifted through the room.

"I hope she made a giant batch of it," Jeff remarked from behind his book.

Pat knew he wasn't reading because she was sure he hadn't turned a page for twenty minutes. Even Jeff wasn't that slow a reader.

"Is your book exciting?" she asked sweetly.

"Oh, very. Very," he replied, turning a page.

"You aren't reading!" Donnie accused.

"How do you know?" Jeff demanded.

"Because I watched your eyes, and they weren't going back and forth, back and forth, like Kurt's and Pat's do when they read. Your eyes just looked straight ahead."

"Go out and see what the fudge is doing, brat," Jeff said good naturedly. After Donnie had gone he turned to Kurt. "That kid's getting too smart for his britches, like Granny says."

Pat went back to thinking about what the teacher had said. If only that teacher *knew* all the things she had to do around the house because she was the only girl! Oh, the boys had work too, but what was that compared to dusting and doing dishes and dull, dull things like that?

Donnie came back. "Now she's beating it," he sang, dancing a happy little jig and knocking over his chair.

"Either sit down and stay *here,* or get out and stay *out.* We're supposed to be able to read," Kurt scolded.

"Donnie, come get the fudge," Mrs. Haley called.

In a minute he was back holding a big plate of luscious looking fudge.

"Be polite, Donnie," Mrs. Haley said from the kitchen. "Pass it around before you take any yourself."

"Ladies first," Pat said, and then was sorry she'd said it because that meant she'd have to be polite and take one of the smaller pieces.

She almost had her hand on one, then froze. Why should she? Why should it always be left to her to take a smaller piece? She moved her hand over the plate and took the biggest one instead.

Kurt and Jeff gasped in horror.

"Donnie passed it to me first, so that gives me the right to the first choice," she said, nibbling on the warm candy.

"Selfish!" Jeff reproached.

"Rude!" Kurt accused.

"Greedy!" Donnie looked for the next biggest piece.

"Even if we took two apiece, we still wouldn't have as much as you," Kurt grumbled.

"Greedy, greedy, greedy!" Donnie was making a little song of it, as if he loved the sound of the word.

Jeff shook his head sorrowfully, "Too bad, but it *is* selfish."

"Greedy, greedy, gree . . ."

Mrs. Haley came to the door. "What's all this shouting about? Your father and I can't hear ourselves think."

Pat had heard her mother say that often, and she thought it was a crazy idea. Why should you try to hear your own thoughts, or, if you wanted to hear each other's thoughts, why not just say them loud enough to be heard over the noise?

"Pat took the biggest piece. She's very selfish and greedy, isn't she, Mom?" Donnie asked.

"And rude," Kurt added.

"Very rude," Jeff agreed, trying hard not to smile.

Pat felt her face get red. Her ears had that awful roaring again.

"I'm getting sick and tired of this. Once,

just *once* I took the first and largest piece, and this is what I've got to put up with. I've always taken the last and smallest piece before. I'm sick of it — sick, *sick,* SICK!"

"Selfish, greedy, greedy!" Donnie whispered it just loud enough for Pat to hear.

"Make him stop that, Mom," Pat cried. "He doesn't even know what it means."

"I do too. It means taking the biggest piece of anything." There was fudge all over Donnie's face.

"Rude." Kurt formed the word without a sound, but Pat saw it.

She put back the rest of her fudge and picked up her library book, too angry to even care if she got fudge on it. She went toward the door.

"Wait!" Mrs. Haley called and turned to face the boys. "I don't think you are being fair to Pat. Just think back. How many times has Pat given in to you in regard to games? How often has she stayed to help me when you fellows had planned baseball games?"

Kurt looked pious. "But isn't that part of being a wo . . . I mean girl? Doesn't the Bible say that . . ."

"Enough!" Mrs. Haley said sternly.

"I think it's time I have a few rights around here," Pat protested. "And it looks like I'm going to have to fight to get them."

"But you're fighting all the time," Kurt said.

"Let's talk this whole thing over, shall we?" Mr. Haley stood at the door.

Pat smiled at him. How wonderful he was! Of course, he had been a boy once too, but he had certainly outgrown it nicely.

Mr. Haley took a piece of fudge and munched it thoughtfully. He licked his fingers and wiped his hands on Mrs. Haley's yellow apron.

"I just had an idea. I think Pat should have one whole day to be utterly selfish. She can think only of herself and her own wishes. How would you like that, Pat? Maybe we can all learn something from that."

"Would I like it? I'd *love* it!" "Boy, would that be a change!" Thoughts raced through her mind. She would take the white meat on the chicken platter and all the liver. She would scrape the bottom of the hard sauce bowl even if Kurt's bread pudding was still bare. After dinner she would walk right out of that dining room without picking up one knife or fork.

"You really mean it? I could do what I wanted for one whole day? The boys would have to play my type games for once?"

"What do you think of that, Mother?" Mr. Haley asked.

"A very good idea. I'm getting a little

tired of these complaints all the time. And Pat might have a few points at that. Since tomorrow is Saturday, let's have it be Pat's day."

"Tomorrow it will be. Boys, did you hear?"

The boys acted like they had just heard they were going to be hanged by their toes in an alligator pit.

"Now, remember," Mr. Haley continued, "no arguments, no reproaches. You will do as Pat wishes. Right?"

"Suppose . . . suppose she would want one of us to jump in the river?" Donnie asked, his eyes wide with fear.

"I'm sure that Pat has better sense than to ask any of you to do something reckless," Mr. Haley said, giving Pat a warning look.

"But she'll give us a bad time – you wait and see," Kurt whispered to Jeff.

"Well, I'm going to bed," Pat announced. "I'll need to be rested for tomorrow. What a day it will be – *what a day!*"

CHAPTER 8

Noises awaken some people, but Pat was always awakened by smells, especially those of food cooking. Saturday morning she jumped awake when she sniffed bacon and pancakes. Then she saw the big blazing ball of sun peeping through the oak leaves and knew it was going to be a lovely day. A great, long, beautiful, selfish day.

Pat heard her father leave for more extra work on that special project. She also heard the boys go downstairs to breakfast. Evidently her mother had called them but was going to let Pat sleep as long as she wanted. But Pat was hungry and, besides, she didn't want to waste another minute of this marvelous day in bed.

The boys were already eating when she came into the kitchen. As soon as her mother saw her, she handed her a plate of pancakes.

"What are your plans for today, dear?" Mrs. Haley asked, pouring some orange juice into a chilled glass.

Pat spread butter between her cakes and poured syrup generously over the stack, even though the pitcher was almost empty. She could feel the boys' reproachful stare, but she enjoyed it. Let them eat sugar on their cakes if the syrup was gone.

"I have a game all planned," she said picking up a fork full of pancakes dripping with syrup.

"Just a minute, dear. The boys can't play all morning. They still have *their* jobs to do. Their father wants them to use the crosscut saw and cut up that dead limb near the fence for fireplace wood for next winter."

"Oh my, yes! We must have firewood," Jeff said. "Please pass the sugar. I see the syrup is all gone."

"Then pass the sugar on to me," Kurt said in a disgusted tone.

"I don't want my pancakes. I don't like sugar on them," Donnie said.

"You *are* eating your pancakes, Donnie," Mrs. Haley said smoothly. "You asked for them, and if you don't like sugar, you can have honey or jelly. Now, boys, I don't want any trouble this morning. Do you hear?"

Pat tried not to feel guilty when she saw her plate still filled with syrup after she'd finished her pancakes. It was a little mean to be too selfish, she decided.

"As soon as the boys are finished with the dead log, you can plan a game with them," said Mrs. Haley. "I'm sure you can entertain yourself until then."

Was her mother being a little sarcastic?

Pat hated to admit it even to herself, but the time that it took the boys to saw up the big log seemed long and empty. They had a game they called Good Guys and Bad Guys. Kurt wrote stories, and then they acted them out in the woods and Granny's old barn. Sam was usually in on these games, but he was still busy painting today. Up till now Pat was never allowed to be the sheriff in these games because she was a girl.

"Did you write a story for today?" she asked Kurt.

"This is *your* day. Remember?" Kurt said shortly.

"Right. I'm going to be the sheriff this time. I'm going to be a beautiful girl-sheriff," Pat announced.

Kurt groaned.

Pat glared at him. "Did you say something, Kurt?"

"No."

"A girl-sheriff? Whoever heard of a dumb girl-sheriff? And you aren't beautiful, Pat, and you . . ."

"Donnie!" Mrs. Haley warned from the house.

"Cut it out, Donnie," Jeff whispered so Mrs. Haley couldn't hear.

"Kurt, you and Jeff can be the bad guys

for a change," Pat directed. "Donnie can be my deputy. Now, we'll give you until I count to a hundred to hide."

The game turned out to be fun — at least for Pat. She had to admit that the boys were really good sports. Sometimes Donnie started to gripe, but Jeff and Kurt always shut him up.

After the game they all went into the house for milk and cookies. Mrs. Haley said the basement had to be cleaned and that the boys would not be available again until the middle of the afternoon.

"I think I'll go for a hike," Pat decided.

"By yourself?" Mrs. Haley said doubtfully.

"I'll take Poochie, and I won't go in the woods. I'll hike up that old dirt road. We haven't been there in ages."

"I'll let you take my dog, but you be careful of him, and if you see any foxes, you grab his collar." Donnie looked stern.

"I'll be home before lunch, and then I've got some games planned for this afternoon when the boys can play," Pat said, stuffing two apples in her jacket pockets.

It was a warm spring day, and she was surprised at the variety of flowers already in bloom. A big bird that Sam had said was a mockingbird sat on a telephone pole and pretended to be every bird he'd ever met. Sometimes his song was sad, and at other times it was a silly clownlike song. He didn't even seem to stop for a breath. Poochie chased the chipmunks and squirrels that dared to cross the road in front of them.

Usually the Haley children turned back at the top of a certain hill, but today was Pat's day and since it was so lovely outdoors, she decided to keep going and fi..d out what was on the other side of the hill. All the countryside was now new to her, and she stopped near a pigpen by the side of the road to look around. She had not seen or heard a person, and she felt wonderfully alone and adventuresome.

A huge mother pig was asleep in an old shed, but her adorable baby pigs were running around near the fence. Pat laughed as she watched them. Poochie was in ecstasies at seeing all those little fat animals chasing around and, suddenly, before Pat could grab him, he'd scooted under the fence and joined the piglets in their play. But the little pigs knew he wasn't one of them. They were terrified and squealed madly.

Pat was afraid one of them might get hurt, so she called Poochie sharply. But he was so excited that he didn't even hear her. Pat finally decided there was nothing she could do except get in that pen and catch the pup. So she climbed over the fence and grabbed for him.

But by this time he was so wild that she couldn't get near him. Then she heard a terrible noise.

It was a grunting, growling, teeth-snapping noise that turned her bones to water. She turned and saw the giant mother pig racing toward them. The monster's little eyes glittered fierce and mean. She went after Poochie first, but he squeezed under the fence just in time and stood quivering on the road.

Then the sow turned and looked at Pat, who stood frozen in terror. There was no way she could make it to the fence in time. The mother pig for all her tremendous size moved fast. Pat had to do something.

A big, half dead tree in the middle of the pen right behind her seemed the only solution, and she shinnied up that tree so fast the boys would have been proud of her. She perched on a limb high enough to be safe and looked down at the raging beast below her. The sow continued to make those horrible teeth-snapping noises. Poochie, outside the pen, squealed and whined along with the baby pigs. The noise was awful.

From her perch, Pat scanned the area for help. It was a lonesome part of the countryside. She saw a house about half a mile away, but she didn't see one living person around it. She realized she'd have to stay up in that tree until

someone came by or the sow decided to go back into her shed.

Time dragged on and on, and Pat grew stiff and tired. She tried to change her position, but the limb she was sitting on gave a warning cracking noise, and she decided to sit very still. She could see herself down in the mud, the big mother pig tearing her to pieces and the baby pigs running up and down and across her helpless body. The thought sent cold shivers down her spine.

"So, this is my beautiful selfish day," she said aloud. "Here I am, spending hours of it above a smelly pigpen, afraid to move for fear I'll be eaten alive. Maybe I'm supposed to get some kind of message from this. Maybe I'm not as unselfish as I think I am." The idea that maybe fat Mrs. Pig was trying to teach her a lesson made her almost hysterical.

"Go back in your pen, please, Mrs. Pig, so I can get down and go home. I believe you— I'm selfish too—and I'll forgive the boys if only I can go home."

Selfish!

Pat thought about that word some more as she tried not to look down at the filthy creature below her. She began to remember some nice things about the boys. What good sports they had been only that morning. How wonderful they had been to her when she had

her tonsils out. Reading to her, playing check-
ers. Jeff had even played paper dolls, although
neither of them had ever breathed a word about
that to Kurt. But Kurt had been great too. He'd
spent all his money on a box of *good* candy,
although, of course, she hadn't been able to
swallow it. Could it be that Patricia Haley was
expecting too much from those three boys? After
all, they weren't saints.

She thought about their doing the breakfast dishes that morning. How they must have
hated that! How they must have hated *her!* That
shook her. She didn't want her brothers to hate
her, because she really loved them. She really
did.

Now she felt miserable inside and out.
It was selfish of her to have walked so far so
that her mother would be worried about her.
No doubt, her mother would soon send the boys
out to look for her. Would they remember that
she said she was coming up this particular road?

She wondered if it was lunchtime yet.
Her empty stomach told her it was, so she moved
slowly and dug the apples out of her pockets. The
old limb didn't crack much, but little noises
warned her not to get too active.

She ate both the apples and threw down
the cores. They hit a little pig who squealed
and started them all crying and running around
again. The sow made more awful teeth-snapping

noises. For a moment Pat could feel her own bones being crunched in that mouth. She looked at Poochie, asleep in the soft warm dust of the road.

"Home Poochie!" she called to him. "Go home. Home, home!" She knew that if the pup went home without her the boys would come looking for her. But Poochie was certainly no "Lassie" of TV fame. He just wagged his little stump of a tail in a friendly way and went back to sleep again.

Pat watched the sun slide down toward the distant hills. Still no one came to the house down the road. "These pigs *have* to belong to someone," she muttered. "Granny says there's money in raising pigs. And pigs have to be fed. Surely someone will show up and feed that horrible old mother and her brats." As her voice rose Poochie opened one eye and listened to her. Then he closed it again.

Then, over the top of the hill, she saw two big boys, a medium-sized boy, and a little one. At that moment she truly loved them. They had come to help her.

CHAPTER 9

"I'm up here in a tree in the pigpen!" Pat screamed. That started the sow off again in a roar of teeth-snapping rage. It suddenly dawned on Pat then how silly she must look, perched up in a dead tree with a mad, fat mama pig guarding her babies against her. Her, Pat Haley, who never stepped on a bug if she could help it! But there she was, high and dry and looking awfully stupid. What if the boys laughed when they saw her? If they dared even to smile, she would just drop down on the ground and let that animal eat her.

But when they came, running fast, not one of them looked anything but worried.

"Don't move, Pat! That limb doesn't look too strong to me," Kurt called.

"Don't worry. We'll get you out of there," Sam added. He was holding Poochie's collar because the dog was getting excited again.

"The limb already cracked once." Pat's voice cracked when she said it.

"Should I run for home and have Mom call Dad?" Jeff asked.

"No, that will take too long," said Kurt. "I don't trust the strength of that limb Pat's on.

Wow! Look at the size of that animal!"

"Yes, and they *are* vicious when they have babies," said Sam. "Too bad we didn't bring a rope. I do believe I could lasso that sow."

"I think you could too, but we don't have a rope, and we don't have too much time." Kurt really looked worried now.

Pat's voice quivered. "If the limb breaks and if . . . well, if something happens to me . . . I want you guys to know that I don't really think you are selfish. I want you to . . ."

Kurt broke in. "Listen, I think I know what might work if you guys are willing."

"Willing to go in and wrestle that animal like in a bull fight?" Jeff asked uncertainly.

"No, you hold Poochie. *Don't* let him get away. And don't let him bark, even if you have to stuff your hand in his mouth. Hear that?"

"Yes, I hear it," Jeff said.

"Now, Sam, you climb the fence, but don't get too far away from it once you get inside. As soon as you get in, yell at the top of your voice so the sow comes after *you*. You willing?

"Wish I had a fancy coat," Sam replied. "Oh, I'll get that old sow after me! When she hears and sees me, she'll come a-running."

"Good. While you're getting her attention, I'll run to the tree and cover for Pat. Pat, as soon as the pig goes for Sam, you jump down and run like mad for the fence."

"But what about you, Kurt? What if she comes after you?" Pat asked.

"I'm a track star, remember? You think all that blubber can outrun *me?* Now, have we got it all straight? Donnie, you find two nice strong sticks."

Pat sat stiff and sore and watched the stage being set around her. Donnie found two sturdy sticks and gave one to Kurt and one to Jeff. Jeff took Poochie in his arms and tried to pet him into another nap. The big scene was about to begin.

Sam swung his long legs over the fence and dropped inside the pen. He was making even worse noises than the mother pig had made. He was also doing a crazy sort of dance. This dance seemed to fascinate the sow, and she just watched him without making a single move. So Sam reached down and grabbed a baby pig.

That did it!

The mother went after Sam with all her teeth grinding and snapping. He leaped for the fence and dropped safely on the other side, the little pig squealing under his arm.

Kurt was now under the limb where Pat sat.

"Run!" he yelled and Pat slid along the limb toward the trunk. There was a loud cracking sound, and she fell in the muck below. When she tried to get up, her legs were so stiff that she fell again. Kurt jerked her up.

"Run," he yelled again, half dragging her toward the fence. Finally her legs began to move.

In the meantime Sam was tickling the baby pig to make it squeal and keep the mother pig's attention. When he saw Pat safely on the other side of the fence, he dropped the baby back into the pen.

"On your own now, track star," he yelled at Kurt.

But by the time the sow had turned to take after Kurt, he was sitting on top of the fence laughing. "Boy, was that fun! Best thing that happened today."

"Not for me," said Pat. "I sat in that dumb tree for hours. It was awful!"

"It's over now," Jeff said. "And Mom has cooked all your favorite things. Granny and Sam will eat with us, and we'll play any game you pick this evening."

"I'll play whatever the majority wants to play," Pat said slowly. "That's more fun than having everything your own way."

Donnie looked at her curiously. "You mean that? You don't think it's fun to be selfish?"

Pat smiled down at him. "Oh, a little selfish maybe. But you can get too much of anything, even selfishness, I guess."